This book is dedicated to every addict, both struggling and in recovery. There is hope. We do recover.

Also for my mother, sweet Melissa, who never got to see me sober. I love you, mommah.

Table of Contents

Wasted

A f*cking genius poetry collection

CiCi Reagan

Edges

It is not a shiny thing,
a room full of coffee cups
and the shakes
and the voices of people telling all the same story
just wrapped up a little different.
it isn't easy.

they come in and out
and you pray to the higher power you created or discovered or
whatever
to please, please don't let that be you
just for one more day. just today.

you white-knuckle that shit at first, though.
you're the one in and out,
the one who makes the people with more than a few days
remember. really remember
how it felt
to not know how to feel.

and the ones with the time,
they thank god it's not them,
and they do what they can,
and they hope that you get it before you die.

these people,
these people with time
[that you think must be lying, cause who can go years without
their vice]
they've heard the sad news and they've been to the funerals.
they have seen and they know
and they see you, and cling ever tighter.

and maybe you see them back,
and you try to hang on, too.
relax those white knuckles, just a little bit.
try to believe in their belief. try not to drown.

then you're writing.
you're writing all the damn time,
and you're powerless,
and stepping,
and now you have to admit
how much you've fucked your life up.
honestly,
you've done a horrible job at just about everything.
but that's alright,
cause you're gonna start over,
you're gonna learn all about yourself.

addicts love that,
we love ourselves.
just usually a more curated version.
so now you learn the truth part.
you keep writing
[and petrify yourself by saying the slogans all the damn time]
and sit in rooms with people you come to love.

you love these people,
the ones who suffer and smile and hug you hello.
you are them,
you know that now.

and even in the middle, there is peace,
like the center of a wake trailing behind a boat.
you just avoid the edges.

Dead Ringer

Last night
I cried
In front of a dozen strangers.

I talked about my father.
I told them
I don't know what to do
With all the emotion.

The last decade
Or longer
Crashes over me-
I am spinning in the current
Blinded by the spray.

I am drowning.

Sobriety is more
Than not drinking.

It's learning how to live again.
How to do things
Without a bottle in your hand.

It's fucking terrifying.

I seem to have the guts.

Maybe I'm just used to trials,
Testing myself,
Adding more accomplishments to the list,
More experiences,
More shit I've overcome.

Some people, though,
Just can't be honest.

They are weak.

My father,
He can't look himself in the eye
And see his flaws,
His shortcomings.
He is comforted by his disorders
[As we all are]
To a point
Where he can't see past them.

A part of me
Recognizes this,
Has sympathy.
A part of me loves him.

Part of me is livid,
Sick of making excuses,
Mad at myself for caring,
Wishing I could shut it off.

I feel this way
Most of the time.
Back and forth
Between acceptance and rage,
Between the fear of and desire to be vulnerable.

I build up my walls
And tear them back down,
Never sure.

I don't know how to forgive,
How to let things go.
Just push it down,
Bury it deep.

My head hurts.
It is a spiral staircase,
Twisting and turning

Going on and on forever.

It's a cemetery
Where the dead are buried
With strings around their wrists
Attached to bells up top
Because they might not
Be truly dead.
I wait for them to awaken.
They never disappoint.

Bleeding Out

Have you ever felt
The urge to escape?

Suddenly,
Fight or flight kicks in

And you don't even know
What you're running from?

Digging my car
Out of the snow
With an umbrella
And my bare hands-
It was like that.

Urgent.

I had to go,
Or implode.
Explode.

If I could have crawled out
Of my own skin,
I would have.

A walking skeleton
With veins and muscles hanging

A graphic, bloody mess,
To let what's inside show.

Do you see me now?

Unkempt
And stumbling blind,
Eyes hanging
From their sockets.

When the world stops spinning,
I see only the floor.

Matted footprints
Show where I've been
Writing a map
To where I am.

Not that you'd want
To join me.
It's messy here,
A jumbled ugliness.

An unfulfilled addiction,
A profound partial insanity
A chasm of unparalleled loss,

An endless emptiness.

Clawing my way
Back up the rabbit hole
Seeing all I missed
On the way down.

Breaking my fingernails,
And splintering bones,
Loosening muscles
And opening veins.

Hurrying a process
I can't rush,
Terrified of bleeding out.

Brains and Pancakes

Painkiller zombies
Fight against the current
Of their syrup-addled brains
With the best of intentions
And poor execution.
Their synapses stuck
In the quagmire
Of unfinished thought
And moving their limbs
Against time and space.
Flustered and impatient
But oh so tired.
Who can blame them
With pancakes for brains?

Wasted

This is why I drink.

I drink because I trust you
And you lie to me
And I'm forced to re-think,
Re-evaluate,
Our entire relationship.

I drink because I hurt.
Painkillers are okay
Because it's my name printed
On the side of the bottle.
But the name I want to see
Is Bombay Sapphire
Wild Turkey 101
Hell, Mad Dog 20/20.
These are my drugs of choice.

I drink because I left him
In one night
Me and my trusty steed
And my getaway bag.
I left my home
And my boys
And never looked back.

I drink because she died.
She was stolen from me
In the ugliest way.
I watched her slowly fade.
Like a lightning bug
On a sticky July night
She lit up
For the last time
And my mother was gone.

I drink because it's easy.

Facing demons is tough shit
And remembering is difficult.
I forgot for a reason.

I drink because he never loved me.
He only loved himself.
He left my sister and I
To tackle life alone.
He imparted no life-lessons,
No fatherly advice.
He vanished, inside a bottle.

It seemed like a good idea
At the time.

I drink to be someone else.
I can forget the world,
My inhibitions,
I can tell you what I really think.
I can sing karaoke
And dance my heart out,
Accept that free drink
From the guy in the cowboy hat.
I can be someone new
The free spirit
In the high-waisted jeans
Taking shots of whiskey
With the big boys.

I drink because
It kills time,
Kills memory,
Kills me.

Sometimes the sun
Shines too brightly
On what I'd rather not see.
So I drink.

Recovered

My hands are dry
From hand sanitizer.
I hate touching things
At hospitals.

The waiting room
Is suffocating.
I'm all sweat
And shaky hands.

Some yards away
Surgeons are removing
The cancer
On my grandmother's kidney.

The family sits
Making small talk-
Jumping at every announcement
And pretending we aren't.

We go through the motions,
Get food in the cafeteria
Take bathroom breaks.
I marvel at the monotony.

In my head, I'm seventeen,
Sitting at my mother's bedside
For months, watching
As she suffers through ALS and pregnancy.

I'm having flashbacks,
I'm there, in my head
PTSD reminding me
Of feelings I'd rather forget.

I'm walking through hallways
Saying hello to nurses.

It smells the same,
And I'm hopeless.

I'm staring into space
Prompting concerned glances
From family members.
I'm fine, I say, I just need air.

I hide out behind a building,
Light a cigarette.
I cannot shake the feeling
That all the happiness
Has been sucked from the world.

A year ago today
I was fighting for my life,
Left homeless
And searching.

Here I sit,
Feeling much the same
As the lifetime ago
Everything changed.
And changed again.

This seems to be the only constant,
Nothing will stay the same,
But always,
I will have myself.

I feel healthy, reinvented
Until I'm hit with the truth
Like a bullet from a .45-
I am damaged.

Someone will walk behind me
And I will flinch, turn away.
I will sit in a hospital
And regress seven years

In mere minutes.

I will want to cry
And find myself too numb for tears,
Reaching for a drink
I shouldn't have.

The surgeons emerge-
Everything went well, they say,
My mema is fine.
I breathe.

I'm exhausted,
I've aged twenty years.
I hold her hand, in her room
An hour later.

Everyone looks so frail
In hospital beds.
I remember everything.
I feel everything.

I find it ironic
That my grandmother
Spent an hour in the recovery room
And after a year of my own,
'Recovered' sounds more like a sick joke
Than anything attainable.

Behind My Eyes

My sleep is plagued by nightmares.
Some are so real
I have to get up,
Walk around,
Check all the clocks,
To convince myself
It didn't happen.

I dream I'm drunk,
Stumbling and unsure,
I've lost my car,
Can't find my cigarettes,
Can't stand up straight.
I fall into walls,
Crawl across the floor,
Inwardly
Hating myself,
Berating myself,
Can't remember where I've been,
How this happened.
I awake,
Disoriented,
Check my phone-
Have I called someone,
Texted someone,
Taken photos-
Where have I been?-
Before I realize
It was only a dream.

A man lurks by my bed,
Watches me as I slumber.
He never speaks.
I know I'm sleeping,
But I'm trapped in my body
Unable to move.
I try to scream

But no sound escapes my lips
I dare myself to move
But I'm frozen.
Sometimes the man moves closer,
Stands right over me.
I can feel him there,
Hooded and dark.
Sometimes he lays down next to me,
I can feel his weight on the bed,
Hear him breathing,
A low growl of his inhales and exhales.
I have the dream over and over
And every time brings him closer.
Last night he touched my hair.
I'm paralyzed
Until I finally awaken,
Shaking
And drenched in sweat.

My mother visits me,
Sick and off-balance.
She raises herself from her hospital bed,
The one she died in,
Her atrophied muscles suddenly working,
But only just.
She moves slowly towards me
On her tiptoes,
Swaying as she goes.
I tell her to stay in bed,
She's going to fall again.
She only moans back at me,
Unable to speak,
And tries to stretch out her arms,
Her fingers gnarled and bent.
Her face is gaunt,
Her skin is dry,
Her bedsores open-
Blood trails behind her as she moves toward me
Ever so slowly.

I move to meet her,
But I'm stuck in quicksand,
Watching her
Until she gets to me.
I open my arms to hold her
And she falls into me.
I'm not strong enough, mommah,
I try to tell her,
But we're falling
And I wake with a start.
Even after death,
Even in dreams,
I cannot save her.

More memories visit me,
Of my ex
Chasing me down the hallway,
Punching holes in the wall
Next to my head.
I hear his friends laughing in the kitchen,
Want desperately to join them,
But he's screaming at me,
I've done something to anger him,
I drink deeply from whatever's in my glass
To brace myself for what's to come.
I'm crying
As he pushes my face into the pillow.
How can he enjoy it if I won't shut up,
He asks me,
And I can't answer,
I hope it'll be over soon.
He gets up,
Asks why it always has to be a fight,
It can't be that bad,
Don't I love him, he has needs.
I'm curled into a ball
And wake up
Wishing I could forget his face,
Forget all the nights

Spent this way.

So I avoid sleep,
Preferring instead to occupy my mind
Until I'm completely exhausted
And hope against hope
That for just a few hours
I'll get a reprieve
From fighting the demons
That live behind my eyes.

Trustworthy

Maybe it's an age thing
Or a woman thing
Or an addict thing
But it's a ludicrous thing
To not know
Your own mind
Or to lack confidence
In your opinions.

I'm always
Looking over my shoulder.
Always asking
What someone else wants,
Or feels, or needs,
Or double checking
That I'm not bothering them
To the point that
I'm sure I am.

I'm conscious of
The way I eat:
How and what and when.

I worry about taking up space-
How close my chair is to the table;
I cross my legs on the metro,
I avoid an occupied kitchen,
Offer to sit in the back of the car,
Even curl into a ball in my own bed.

Where do I want to go?
Anywhere is fine.
Am I hungry?
I don't know- are you?

I want to contribute without pressure,
I want to help without demand.

I concern myself with the needs of others,
Hell-bent on being understanding, sweet, kind,
And aware of boundaries;
Skirting around the edges
Listening from the sidelines for opinions,
Studying body language
And asking for advice.

Am I over reacting?
I ask myself.
Am I just tired or hormonal or hungry-
Do I really feel the way I feel
Or is it just a symptom of something else?
No point making waves,
I say,
Over something so trivial.

But if it is so trivial,
Why have I hidden myself in the bathroom
To succumb to tears?

And why do I hide?
Is it necessary
To shield myself from sight
Before I can let go
Of this stony exterior,
Even just a little bit?
Do other people
Sit on the couch in their living room
And have a good cry
In front of someone?
Is that a thing that happens?

Is it okay to ask someone
Not to throw their hat in anger
Over a football game-
Because that behavior scares me,
Because it brings up the past?

Is it fair of me
To pin that fear,
To pin my issues,
On them?

Can I ask a new friend
To please not drink in front of me
Because I'm white-knuckling my sobriety
As it is
And at any moment
I could fall into that bottle of Tanqueray
And drown?

Should I say what I want to say
When I hear judgmental voices
About things that matter to me?
Should I be that voice I'd want to hear
And stand up for those
Who need a voice?
Stand up for myself?

Is it alright
That I am this way-
Empathizing with others,
Taking on their pain,
Internalizing their conflict
And stressing myself out?
Is that a good thing-
Or something I should try and change?

And why do I need
To ask these things-
Why do I reach out to the universe,
The internet,
My family,
For validation of my own opinions?

I used to be much more sure,
When I was younger.

How interesting that
Even though I had less experience,
I trusted myself.
I went with every gut instinct;
I didn't fight my own mind.
I got myself into trouble, sure,
But I wasn't in a self-inflicted cage.

Maybe I'll find me
Somewhere in the middle
Of these opposing ideas.
Maybe I needn't be so extreme.

I don't know
How much of my thoughts are my own,
Or my addiction's,
Or the echoing voices of those who've hurt me.

I wonder if I am trustworthy.

Existential Global Positioning

I smell like the store
I bought this shirt from.
It reeks of
Instant gratification.

I want a cigarette
But my coffee cup is empty
And anyway
It's cold out there.

I stare at the people outside
And pretend their nicotine
Is for me.

I found the historic part of this town:
My GPS directed me,
Via satellite,

Back in time.
Original flooring
Holds up the humans
In plaid flannel shirts,

[Me included,]

And original brickwork
And fairy lights
And stone steps
And tattoos.

I am obsessed by time
And juxtaposition
And where I fit.

Cities are too big,
Skies void of stars,
And one horse towns

Far too small.

I am
The wrong size
For both.

My ideas
Are too large for my brain
And too ahead
Of my current location.

I can cross
A hundred time zones
In buses, planes, and cars,
But I always find me:

Unimpressed,
Unimportant,
Out of my place
In time.

The music plays,
Throaty and breathless,
All acoustic guitars
And steel drums.

People converse
Over raspberry mochas
And hot chocolates
Saying nothing.

I write,
Glasses off,
Moving my hair, my pen,
Saying nothing-

Nothing
I haven't already said
A million times

In a billion poems.

Seconds go by
And eternities,
Completely unnoticed.

We measure time
By accomplishments
By worthiness
By cups of coffee.

What do we have
To show for ourselves?

New years are celebrated,
Januarys full of hope
And commitment
And fresh starts.

Our commutes
Are measured in miles,
Our successes by how far we've moved
From where we grew up.

I receive aluminum tokens
Symbolising days without drinks.
People clap.

I make tentative plans
For uncertain futures
And the barista wishes exiting patrons
A good night.

We might even mean it.

I am baffled
By years and seconds
And how to measure my life
And wonder

If there's ever a time
When the stars,
The satellites,
Will tell us:

You have arrived
At your destination.

Erasing

they said i am a joy.
they see me through eyes
unknowing and brand new-
i am competent, and capable.

i used to watch Home Improvement
with my father.
he said it was funny,
so it was.
i thought what he thought.

i was adorable on demand.

i was lots of things on demand
for lots of people.
i took requests.

i watched the fire burn,
watched them drive away,
watched her die,
watched them (the collective him) hurt me

all from outside myself.

scapegoat, whipping post,
ball of rage,
on demand.

all or nothing.

i was
failed perfection,
clean house and dirty hair,
obsessively wiping down the kitchen counters
freeing them of the condensation rings from the tiny glasses
between every shot.
erasing.

alcoholic housewife
on demand.

it took me years to realize
i don't particularly like Home Improvement
and i'm not a version of myself,
a stripped-down section
for easier consumption,
layerless.

i have opened the boxes
i hid myself in
i have stared inside
and weeped
at what i have seen.
i have cast light across the shadow.

i no longer take requests.

My Depression Has a Soundtrack

My depression has a soundtrack.

It sounds like a racing heart,
So fast that nurses hook me to machines
Just in case. Just to check.

It sounds like
Music blaring in my ears while I walk through town,
The Cranberries and Amy Winehouse and The Dresden Dolls
Serenade me
As I pretend I'm someone else.

It's a constant barrage
Of 'why didn't I do more'
Mixed with 'I can't get out of bed.'

It's a dirty house and an empty fridge,
The sound of the boiler pumping out heat
While I sit on the couch and shake.

It's constant noise-
YouTube videos I don't want to watch,
Podcasts I'm not interested in,
Shows and movies I've seen a hundred times.
A barrage of information,
Just to keep my own mind quiet,
To keep myself out of the dark.

It's the voices of friends,
Of doctors,
Giving out advice and prescriptions,
'Try this,' they say.
'Try that.'

It sounds like heavy breathing,
Fast in and out,

After waking from a nightmare,
Sweaty and petrified,
Because even in dreams,
There is no escape.

It's my phone vibrating,
Telling me about messages and missed calls,
While I sit and stare,
Too overwhelmed by my own existence
To respond.

It's a scream
Of frustration, exhaustion, and fear.
Trying my best and not being enough,
A prisoner inside my own mind,
Pounding on the walls of my skull,
Begging for freedom.

I'm CiCi Reagan-

a poet, recovering alcoholic, and domestic abuse survivor.

I got sober on January 1st, 2016. Before and since, life has been a hell of a roller coaster. I've written during panic attacks in the depths of addiction, and while riding the pink cloud in early recovery. It's all real, it's sometimes shit, sometimes great, and it all passes.

I've written about others' addiction as well, such as growing up with an alcoholic father, and the ongoing ripples that effect the lives of myself and my family to this day.

I hope that my experience can help others, including those fighting their own battles with addiction or family members of addicts. Addiction isn't easy to understand, and it tears lives apart, but there is always hope. Anyone can change if they want to.

Praise for CiCi Reagan's Poetry

"Profound.
Beautiful.
Moving."
-Dana Swift

"I am always delighted to read you. you don't miss a beat."
-Nita Harris

" You are such talented writer."
-Karen Garner

" You are an excellent writer. Few people can put their pain
into words as artfully as you do."
-Liz Ryan

" I am always inspired by you."
-Jess Strickland

Featured on

Thrive Global
The Inspiration North Podcast
The Change it Up Podcast

Printed in Great Britain
by Amazon